RESCUED in AMERICA

melissa mcdaniel

the photo book projects: book 2

the
photo book
projects

PRESENT DOG
P R E S S

RESCUEDinAMERICA | the photo book projects | melissa mcdaniel

published in 2010 by present dog press

www.melissashouse.com
www.thephotobooks.com

the
photo book
projects

ISBN-13: 978-0-9845903-1-5
ISBN-10: 0-9845903-1-5

designer: melissa mcdaniel

printer: colorado printing

the text of this book was composed in helvetica cy

printed and bound in USA
10 9 8 7 6 5 4 3 2 1

PRESENT DOG
P R E S S

present dog press, po box 454, new hope, pa 18938 | www.presentdogpress.com

for my grandmother Elsymae Shepperd and my grandfather Tom Shepperd
who passed on to me their great love and compassion for animals;
for my deaf dog Sadie
who taught me that no disability is limiting if you refuse to acknowledge it as such
and that no moment is better savored than the one that is happening right now;
for Egil Nilsson
whose unwavering support of the projects took him to places he probably wished he'd never seen;
for all of the dogs who were never lucky enough to find their forever homes

Dogs should be treated as individuals and should not be stereotyped by their breed, their "handicap" or their past. Judge them for who they are, not for what others have told you they are.

Melissa McDaniel

introduction

here's to a day when all pets have a loving and safe place to call home

I walked into a small shelter in a rural New Mexico town expecting nothing different from what I had seen in shelters and rescues in other cities and towns on our trip up until that point. We had been on the road for almost a month—me, Egil (my other half) and our two dogs, Sadie and Bella—traveling the country to take photos for this book and another photo book, *Deaf Dogs*. We had been photographing participants' dogs in their homes, and that day, we had found ourselves an hour early for our appointment. The woman whose dogs I would be photographing suggested I visit this shelter, since she had adopted her dog there years earlier. By that point on our trip, I had visited Humane Societies, SPCAs, small local rescues and small breed-specific rescues—all low-kill or no-kill facilities. I had talked to their employees and volunteers. It was the same everywhere. Due

to the economy, intake numbers were up, donations were down and shelters were understaffed. We talked about the common reasons for relinquishment, about the types of animals they see most, about our own dogs and about the photo books. Those visits were pleasant, but my visit that day in New Mexico was not. I guess if I had known where I was going, I would have had a different mindset, but I didn't know. I was headed into local animal control.

The building was old. The walls were dark. I told the two women in the office what I was doing and asked if I could photograph some of the dogs. They were reluctant at first, but then let me through. I walked into the dog area, which was small, but each kennel contained several dogs. The dogs were cute and friendly, but stressed. I took their photos and returned to the office to speak to the women. It was then I heard the grim news. They pointed to some statistics that hung on the wall. The number of dogs brought in to the shelter last year was slightly over 3,000. The number that made it out, was just over 300. The dogs I had just photographed had a 10 percent chance of making it out alive. Six to seven dogs were put down daily. Dogs were given a set number of days and then were euthanized. It didn't matter if there was space or not, their time was up.

I'm not singling out this state or this shelter. Dogs are euthanized in shelters in every state, every day. It's not uncommon for shelters in large cities to admit 10,000 to 30,000 dogs per year. The Mayor's Alliance for NYC's Animals, reports that 42,000 cats and dogs enter New York City's shelter system each year, and 33 percent of those animals were euthanized in 2009. That means 67 percent were adopted or reunited with their families.

The Humane Society of the United States (HSUS) estimates that between six and eight million cats and dogs enter shelters each year, and of those, three to four million are euthanized (other groups estimate that the numbers are far higher). These numbers pale in comparison to the dark days of the 1970s, when as many as 20 million dogs and cats were euthanized each year. This drastic decrease in numbers is largely due to the effectiveness of spay-and-neuter campaigns across the country. In certain areas of the country, these campaigns have been so effective that shelters in those areas no longer need to euthanize animals due to lack of space. Many of those shelters with available space work with rescues and shelters in areas of the country where these campaigns haven't been as effective, and transport animals from the overpopulated high-kill shelters, to their uncrowded facilities, where animals stand a greater chance of finding a home.

Spay and neuter your pets. Spaying and neutering is the best way to control the pet population and to decrease the number of animals euthanized in shelters each year. For this reason, I am an active supporter of low- and no-cost spay and neuter programs that work to decrease the number of homeless pets. I have had people tell me that they want their dog to have "just one litter" before they spay her. If you let your dog have just one litter, the HSUS estimates that your dog's offspring, within six years, theoretically could produce 67,000 dogs (based on a female dog's ability to have two litters of six to 10 puppies per year).

Dogs are for life. For a few months in 2008, I volunteered at my local animal shelter. I wanted to give back to the shelter from which I had adopted my dog Sadie six years earlier. I took photographs of the animals, to help promote them on the shelter's website, and walked the dogs. While I knew this country had a pet overpopulation problem, it was at the shelter that I soon learned that this country also has a pet-retention problem (*see text box*). When you adopt a dog, you are making a commitment to that animal, but unfortunately, many people don't see it that way.

Most dogs are in shelters through no fault of their own. While many of the dogs at the shelter were brought in as strays, many more were owner surrenders, and the reasons for relinquishment were surprising: the owners were moving, they had lost their jobs, they didn't have time for a dog, they were getting a divorce, etc. Contrary to popular belief, most people surrender their dogs to shelters for reasons other than "my dog misbehaves." In an American Humane survey of 93 shelters across the country, "moving" was the most common reason given by owners for relinquishing a pet.

At the time, when I told clients and friends that I was volunteering at the shelter, many thought it was wonderful, but some commented that they would never adopt a shelter dog themselves, because "you never know what you're going to get." Whenever they said that, I would think of all the great dogs I had seen that week at the shelter. I knew some people's beliefs and concerns about shelter and rescue dogs simply weren't valid. These common misconceptions were interfering with some great dogs getting great homes. That was when I decided to start this book.

Since I knew I was already going to be traveling across the country to photograph dogs for the photo book *Deaf Dogs* (Sadie is deaf), I thought I could at the same time photograph rescued dogs. All of the dogs in this book, at one time homeless, have found their forever homes; they were either adopted from shelters or rescues or were found as strays. All of the dogs are now cherished members of their families, and their people couldn't imagine life without them. It was important for me to include only dogs that had found their forever homes because **I wanted the dogs' stories to show the readers what I already knew firsthand: rescued dogs make great pets.**

7

Word spread quickly that I was doing this project, and the book started to fill up with participants. I had no application process; it was just first come, first serve. I was happy to include dogs that didn't have sad histories, because I wanted the book to show that there are many great dogs with no issues, with no history of abuse—some extremely well-trained—sitting in shelters and rescues across the US. (At my local shelter, I remember a beautiful Border Collie, trained in agility; his owners dropped him off because they were moving.) I did worry that my open-door policy toward prospective participants would result in a book filled with one breed or another, but I was pleasantly surprised. By chance, I ended up with a nice mix of dogs. There are a large number of pit bulls and pit bull mixes, but I think this accurately represents the situation in most US shelters, since pit bulls are the number one most-bred dog "breed," at the moment, due to backyard breeders.

Open your mind to pit bulls. I put "breed" in quotes because the term "pit bull" is applied to various breeds (and even mixes). There is a breed called American Pit Bull Terrier, however, any dog, purebred or mixed, with a certain look is labeled a "pit bull." Pit bulls and pit bull mixes were the breed most seen at my local shelter. I have to say I had had little experience with pit bulls before I volunteered there, and was slightly intimidated by their reputation. However, after days of meeting pit bull after pit bull that wanted nothing more than to wag his or her tail and lick my face, I quickly changed my mind. I remember all too well walking well-trained, gorgeous, smart, full-of-love dogs at the shelter and getting approached by potential adopters who clearly fell in love with the dogs, but who would then immediately stop petting the dogs and back away when they found out they were pit bull mixes. In reality, most of these dogs are smart, eager to please, easy to train, lovable goofs whose media and public reputation so greatly contrasts with their actual demeanor, it's shocking.

At the moment, they are being bred by irresponsible backyard breeders all across the US at an alarming rate and shelters are overrun with them. Pit bulls are among the first to be euthanized in kill shelters because the shelters know they are harder to adopt out than other breeds. Statistics on the Missouri Pit Bull Rescue's website say that 40 percent of dogs in US shelters are pit bulls, and for every one pit bull that is adopted, 599 are put down. An estimated 75 percent of US shelters do not adopt out pit bulls; all pit bulls and pit bull mixes entering those shelters are euthanized. The modern plight of these dogs is truly tragic.

I had many reasons why I wanted to create this book, but more than anything else I wanted to give back to my dog Sadie, a former shelter dog who has given me so much. I often wonder what would have happened to her if I hadn't shown up that day. When I adopted Sadie, she was just 4 months old and had been surrendered to the shelter, along with her littermates because the owners could not afford to keep them. The owners had not spayed their dog and the litter was an "accident." Sadie was at the shelter for 90 days before I adopted her. Once Sadie was spayed, I took her home. She spent the entire car ride sleeping in the passenger seat resting her head in my lap.

I will never forget those walks during the first month I had Sadie. She would take a few steps, look up at me until I looked down at her and then she would walk a little further and then look at me again. She kept doing this. With her content look and her tail wagging, she seemed to be making sure I was still there, and also thinking, "Are you really mine?" She only kept that up for a few weeks, but I'll never forget it. I now understand why she did what she did. Sadie needs a person. She likes to be with me, follows me from room to room, likes to have a job, and, being deaf, she checks in with me often. I can't help but think she must have felt lost those first few months before she found me. So when people say they would never rescue a dog because "you never know what you're going to get," I remember those first few walks with Sadie, and I think, "I know exactly what you're going to get. Gratitude and love."

I often think of those dogs I saw in that New Mexico shelter and realize how easily any of the dogs in this book could have suffered a similar fate—if they had been born in a different town, had been adopted by people who viewed them as disposable, hadn't been trained or given a stable home life, or any other number of reasons. It wasn't the dogs' fault they were in that New Mexico shelter, it was the fault of some person somewhere who didn't get their dog fixed, who didn't take the time to train their dog, who let their dog wander the neighborhood, who didn't put identification on their dog, who didn't view their dog as family.... The owners of those dogs probably didn't say or even think, "I don't want this dog anymore. You can just kill him." However, this is what ultimately happened. If I had known what I was walking into that day, perhaps it wouldn't have had such an impact on me (after all, I'd been in animal control facilities before). I expected to be walking into a low-kill rescue, and so the contrast between what I expected to see and what I did see seemed all the more striking. The wasteful disposal of America's animals was right there in front of me.

Millions of animals are euthanized in shelters each year and most people accept this as the way it has to be. My overwhelming thought when I consider the fate of those dogs in New Mexico and the fate of millions of dogs in shelters across the US is, "it doesn't have to be this way." We've turned our backs on our most loyal companions. The good news is that things are changing. There is a large no-kill movement in this country, led by people hoping to end the euthanasia of unwanted pets in the US. Spay and neuter campaigns are working. Euthanasia numbers are decreasing. These facts give hope to all dogs in the future, who find themselves, like the dogs in this book once did, homeless through no fault of their own.

RESCUED
in AMERICA

jesse james

samantha

minnie

14

twinkie

15

twinkie

16

francisco

17

sundance kid

cici

archibald bo macleod

lil' britches

taffy

charlie

23

lacy hannah & remy martin

lacy hannah & remy martin

yoda

ziggy

frankie

28

vanna

max

30

ce-ce

itsey

johann

nicholas ivan

34

gracie

angus

36

chaos

stevie

martin

winnie

mabel (wiberg)

ripley (long ayscue)

wrangler

gretchen

44

uno

eva

bailey

47

sampson

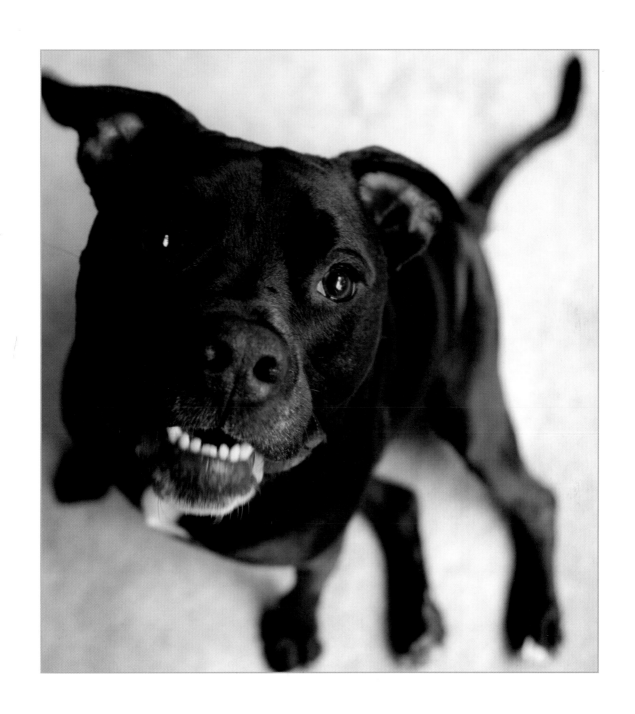

brady

zip

doc

ripley (tuthill)

bosco

jaeger

gryffin

hector

carbon copy

58

sunny

59

dena

dena

61

nittany

henry

sawyer

lucy

65

lady (bond)

chloe

heartland's magnolia

mabel (bennett-mitchell)

murphy

hank

bandit

bonnie

74

lucie

75

tucker (fanelli)

porter

ginger

memphis

monty

independence

katie

82

mudd puppy

mimi

84

zeke

ace

madonna (& pups)

rufus

88

jessie

jeep

lady (mcnamara-miller)

miracle houdini

wilfredo

93

harley

heike

willow & zipping thru the darkside

willow & zipping thru the darkside

harry & darcy

98

daisy & bella bean

roxy

100

woodrow

franklin

rocky

maude

104

lady (vijay)

natasha

shania

penny

jasper

110

toby

tye

112

jakera

blue eyes

pezziwig

tucker (bartlett-sullivan)

116

phoenix

phoenix

lydia lamb

120

sadie

THE STARS of the RESCUEDinAMERICA photo book

The source of most quotes in the biographies has been omitted; the quotes were made by the people mentioned in the bios that are owned by these dogs. If a dog lives with another dog that did not come from the same litter, the dog is referred to in quotes as the dog's "sister," "brother" or "sibling." If the dogs are actual littermates or blood relatives, then there are no quotation marks around mother, sister, brother, etc. Some of the participants asked that only their first name be used, and so their surnames have been omitted. If one breed is listed for a dog, then the dog is believed to be a purebred. If 'mix' is listed after the breed, then the dog is most likely made up of the breeds listed, although it is sometimes just a best guess.

ace
aka ace monster, he loved to roam the farm & sunbathe on the porch
great dane
elverson, pa
pulled from a georgia high-kill shelter by second time around rescue (star)

Heidi Sydlosky, through her rescue STAR, pulled Ace from a Georgia shelter. Ace was found as a stray after his owners, in trouble for not feeding him, let him loose. He went to Heidi's and never left. Almost bald from malnourishment, he took six months to go from 85 to a healthy 135 lbs. "He turned out to be the best and most beautiful dog." Ace, who loved everyone and everything, sadly passed away in 2010 from kidney failure.

angus
aka angusbobangus, he loves & does extremely well at agility
american pit bull terrier mix
san clemente, ca
adopted from canine crusaders

Kristen (*see Lil' Britches & Sampson*) was looking to adopt a pal for her dog Sampson when a friend told her about a young male found roaming in South Central LA. Angus and Sampson met at the dog park and have been best buddies ever since. Expressive and emotional Angus communicates with a variety of whines, moans, sighs and howls. He loves to run in the hills and adores kids. "Licking a kid's face is his main goal in life!"

archibald bo macleod
aka archie, he is lovable & gentle, & loves watching lizards on the back porch for hours
border collie
austin, tx
adopted from his previous owner

Archie spent the first two years of his life crated outside until a co-worker of Therese Kopiwoda (*see Lydia Lamb*) convinced his owner to surrender Archie to her. The woman brought Archie to work the next day, and Archie followed Therese around like her shadow, making it clear that he had chosen her. "Once I looked into his eyes, it was all over. He immediately owned a piece of my heart and came home with me that day!"

bailey
aka bailey boo, boo, booey & bunny, she loves people & is very gentle with kids
rottweiler mix
scottsdale, az
adopted from arizona humane society (ahs)

Two-year-old Bailey, surrendered because her home's kids teased her, and she wasn't good with dogs, was on AHS's Pets on Parade TV show. Dylan & Susannah Fields saw her and knew she was theirs. Others had seen the show and had wanted her, too, so AHS held a lottery, and Bailey went home with the Fieldses. A "gentle giant," Bailey just wants the love and praise she was denied at her first home. She gets that—and more!

bandit

aka punkin & keerp; sleeps in a "dead bug" position—on his back with his feet in the air
catahoula leopard dog mix
lancaster, sc
adopted from saving the animals of rowan (star)

Slated to be put down at a Kentucky shelter for being "unadoptable" due to extreme shyness, Bandit owes his life to STAR for pulling him. Rebecca Steen adopted him, not knowing he was sick with worms, coccidia, anemia and a respiratory infection. Obedient Bandit is now healthy and confident; Rebecca continually receives compliments on what a sweet, calm dog he is. He loves to play with and hide under towels and blankets.

bella bean

loves wresting & playing with, & has brought new life to, her older "sister" stevie
yorkshire terrier
morrisville, pa
adopted from bucks county spca (bcspca)

In 2009, the BCSPCA rescued 46 Yorkies (*see pg. 149*) from an illegal puppy mill. Three of the dogs were pregnant, including one (*see Darcy*) who gave birth to Bella Bean and another girl (*see Daisy*). John, Debbie, Amanda & John M. Dubell (*see Stevie*) adopted Bella. She now has a great home where she chases squeaky balls, wrestles with "sister" Stevie and goes camping. She gets to visit her dad (*see Harry*) and sister Daisy often.

blue eyes

a snuggle bug, he loves running in the countryside, playing with other dogs & car rides
catahoula leopard dog
harrisburg, pa
pulled from a virginia high-kill shelter by catahoula rescue inc (cri)

When Abbey Lewis went to Blue's CRI foster home to adopt him, Blue hid behind his foster mom and trembled when Abbey got close. Found as a stray, no one is sure what happened in his previous life, but he is terrified of crates and has had to learn to trust people. He wouldn't leave Abbey's home for the first week; she had to carry him out. He is still wary of strangers and new places. "He is a total lovebug, but it's on his terms."

bonnie

loves running with kate's mare; they nap together & bonnie uses the mare as a pillow
american staffordshire terrier
elko, nv
found in a dumpster in 20-degree weather

At just 1 week old, Bonnie was stuffed in a cardboard box and left to die in a dumpster. This "throwaway dog" has become a cherished service dog and companion for Kathryn Bales...and it was all Bonnie's idea. Kate was trying to train a Rottweiler to be her service dog. When the dog didn't respond to Kate's request to get the phone, 4-month-old Bonnie stepped in and brought it to her. Bonnie has been Kate's service dog ever since.

bosco

this bird dog finally discovered birds & now runs through flocks under the bird feeder
american brittany
cleveland, oh
adopted from american brittany rescue (abr)

Bosco's owner brought him to a vet after an "accident" broke Bosco's leg. Since he didn't have the money to set his leg, his owner had Bosco's leg wrapped, however, the owner didn't care for it properly and gangrene set in. That's when ABR intervened, and Laura & Andrew Bernhard adopted Bosco. Playful Bosco had his leg amputated, but lives life on three legs as though he had four. He loves chasing the cat and cuddling.

brady

loves everyone & everything, including the home's bearded dragon & new puppy
american pit bull terrier mix
gainesville, fl
adopted from a kill shelter in south florida

Kandin Kogler & Kevin Rutter rescued Brady from a kill shelter in South Florida, unaware that Brady had severe hip dysplasia and was heartworm positive. He loves to run and swim, but his activity needs to be limited or he will be immobile for days afterward. Brady loves the vacuum cleaner; he follows it around the house while Kandin is cleaning and sits next to it when she is done. Brady helps transition the home's many foster dogs.

carbon copy

aka carby & the carbster, he follows around & acts as nanny for the little girl next door
the rare irish potato hound (or possibly golden retriever-boxer-rottweiler mix)
saratoga springs, ny
adopted from a rescue in missouri; seen on dogsindanger.com

Justine Blair Carroll received a call from Jami & Hugh Chandler requesting training help for their dog Carby, whom they had saved from being euthanized in a Missouri shelter after seeing him on DogsinDanger.com. His issues included, but were not limited to, escaping, digging, destructive chewing, barking and leash aggression. Justine turned him around, taking him to her home on occasion, and then later keeping him for good.

ce-ce

aka squirt, she is a known sock thief & squirrel chaser
chihuahua
baltimore, md
given away for free online

June & Terry Bond (*see Chloe & Lady*) adopted Ce-Ce after seeing her advertised on a local website as "free to a good home." Her original owners didn't want her any longer, and the Bonds knew they could give her a great home with their three other dogs. Ce-Ce loves to follow Terry everywhere—all over the house and yard. She developed epilepsy two years ago, but she still remains "a very happy girl."

chaos
aka "k" & buddy; will walk on his hind legs to get to a counter or treat; squirrel chaser
jack russell terrier-fox terrier mix
seymour, ct
adopted from animals for life (afl)

Chaos was brought to AFL at 8 weeks of age after his owners realized he wasn't a purebred. He soon came down with parvo and almost died, and his front left leg needed to be amputated after a dog bite. Marc & Debbie Maas adopted him as soon as they saw him. Survivor Chaos loves life. "We believe Chaos thinks he has four legs." A social butterfly who wants to be where the action is, Chaos "talks" more than he barks.

charlie
loves kids & the dog beach; he can calm aggressive dogs almost instantly
terrier mix
huntington beach, ca
adopted from orange county humane society (ochs)

Joan Wheeler's daughter, who had been volunteering at the OCHS walking dogs, sent a picture of Charlie to Joan's cell phone, and that was all it took to make Joan rush to the OCHS and adopt him. Of Charlie's history, Joan only knows that he had been found on the streets of Westminster, California, "but every day I am amazed that...someone let this wonderful companion get away." Lucky Charlie is now "the King of the Household."

chloe
aka clo-clo, she loves to go on walks & play in the rain
german shepherd-labrador retriever mix
baltimore, md
adopted from partnership for animal welfare (p.a.w.)

June & Terry Bond (*see Ce-Ce & Lady*) went to visit Chloe, who, they were told, was timid and needed socialization. However, when the Bonds went to meet her, she came to them without any fear. They adopted her. She is shy around new people, but has been a "gentle joy" in the Bond household. Chloe acts as the ears and "big sister" to their deaf dog Angel and is certified for Pets on Wheels to visit the elderly.

cici (short for cookies & cream)
aka kooky, koo koo, rooky, nini & li'l meatball, she loves the ocean & snuggling
papillon mix
san clemente, ca
rescued off the streets of fajardo, puerto rico

Denise Swift (*see Francisco, Twinkie & Wilfredo*) leaped into traffic to save this little malnourished puppy, who was scared and suffering from mange. Cici flew to California and was placed with a family that loved her, but they were away too much to care for her. She moved in with Cory Swift & Neil Russell (*see Max & Vanna*) and stayed. Smart Cici can fetch different toys by name, smile on command and mimic you when you dance.

daisy

she was born in a shelter, but now has a loving home
yorkshire terrier
penndel, pa
adopted from bucks county spca (bcspca)

In 2009, the BCSPCA rescued 46 Yorkies (*see pg. 149*) from an illegal puppy mill. Three of the dogs were pregnant, including one (*see Darcy*) who gave birth to Daisy and another female (*see Bella Bean*). Brian McShane adopted Daisy and gave her a great home. She gets to visit her dad (*see Harry*) and sister Bella Bean often.

darcy

loves car rides & giving kisses; "she is a happy little dog & has given us so much joy"
yorkshire terrier
langhorne, pa
adopted from bucks county spca (bcspca); a former puppy-mill dog

Robert & Harriet Halliday adopted Darcy after she was pulled from an illegal puppy mill (*see pg. 149*). The Hallidays were excited to bring Darcy home, but when she was found to be pregnant (*see Bella Bean & Daisy*), they had to wait another three months before she could be adopted from the BCSPCA. She adapted quickly to her new home and is now best friends with the Hallidays' cat Simon. "We could not have a nicer dog."

dena

a hello bully "spokes-bull" who educates the public about dogs labeled as "pit bulls"
american pit bull terrier
pittsburgh, pa
adopted from animal friends; works for hello bully (hellobully.com)

Amy Dengler (*see Porter*) adopted 1-year-old Dena from Animal Friends. Dena had been confiscated from owners who were later convicted of neglecting her and several other pit bulls. Thin and unsocialized, Dena had been chained outside and never taken indoors. She is proof that dogs shouldn't be labeled and should be treated as individuals. Never dwelling on the past, she adores everyone she meets and has no trust issues.

doc

trains in schutzhund & knows commands in english & german
american pit bull terrier
baltimore, md
adopted from his previous owner

Chained outside by an Alabama pit bull breeder and then pulled at the 11th hour by a rescue, Doc was shuffled between foster homes and adopted out (but returned) before Erin Sullivan & Rob Bartlett (*see Tucker*) fostered him. Erin taught him manners. Realizing that this difficult dog really needed stability, they adopted him. Obsessed with food, Doc is often seen staring at the treat jar, aka "Praying to the Biscuit Gods."

eva

loves smiling & "breakdancing" (wiggling around, scratching her back on the floor)
american pit bull terrier mix
batesville, va
adopted from her previous owner; courtesy posted online by animal connections

Eva lived with a family that was moving. The family was going to have Eva euthanized after their new homeowner's association banned Eva because she was "an aggressive breed," but luckily someone stepped in to save her. She was eventually adopted by Arin Bennett & Ashley Mitchell (*see Mabel & Monty*). Eva loves to both wrestle with her new "brothers" and "sister" and keep them in line. She loves kids and loves to cuddle.

francisco

aka mugs & the hamburgler since he will "leap tall buildings" to get to food
shih tzu mix
monterey, ca
found as a stray

Denise Swift (*see Twinkie & Wilfredo*) found Francisco in her backyard one day. He was emaciated, matted and covered in sores. Since he had no id tags, he was kept at the local shelter on hold in case his original owners were still looking for him. Denise visited him daily and as soon as he was made available for adoption, she took him home. Francisco is now a therapy dog who is well-trained, obedient and loves food.

frankie

aka bean, she's a happy, well-adjusted girl who likes to work on her tan
terrier mix
oceanside, ca
found as a stray at a garbage dump in puerto rico

Found thin, shy and mangy in Puerto Rico by Denise Swift (*see Francisco, Twinkie & Wilfredo*), Frankie was flown to the US and met Charity Smith on Valentine's Day; Charity wasn't sure what to expect from Frankie, her first dog. "She has been a tangible blessing in my life," and was the impetus for Charity's advocacy and rescue work—loveisthepits. com. Frankie loves to go on walks and will eat or roll in the ickiest thing she can find.

franklin

franklin & "brother" rocky are affectionately referred to as "the hounds"
beagle, possibly beagle-jack russell terrier mix
philadelphia, pa
adopted from almost home animal shelter (almost home)

Found as a stray, Franklin was adopted from Almost Home by Catherine & Charles Rombeau (*see Rocky*), who think, because he can jump 5 feet straight in the air to lick people's faces, that is he part JRT. While Franklin has bursts of energy and agility that would make any athlete jealous, he also competes with Rocky to see who is the better sleeper. His loving, bouncy personality captures the heart of everyone who meets him.

127

ginger
loves wrestling with her "siblings" & going on camping trips
american pit bull terrier
sioux falls, sd
adopted from pit rescue of the great plains (prgp)

Clint Miller, Jennifer McNamara & daughter Casey Miller (*see Lady*) adopted Ginger from PRGP. Ginger's entire litter was surrendered to the rescue at birth. The family fostered and adopted her immediately, so her entire life has been with them. "All of our dogs have been rescued. None show any lingering signs of their past. They are happy, healthy pets who love us and each other."

gracie
aka lady grace; a great watchdog, snuggler & lovebug, sweet gracie loves people
border collie mix
tallahassee, fl
adopted from new england border collie rescue (nebcr)

Surrendered to a Michigan shelter after her owners' divorce, Gracie was then adopted by a couple who decided they didn't want her around their child. NEBCR saved her. Her NEBCR foster home was the son and daughter-in-law of Rosemary Bryant, who would be the one to adopt Gracie. Everyone comments on how sweet Gracie is. She loves games, including bowling for treats, but most of all she loves just being with Rosemary.

gretchen
herds chickens on command; loves to lie by the fire & to tease her "brother" with toys
rottweiler
racine, wi
adopted from a milwaukee shelter; health issues believed to be from bad breeding

Found abandoned in a house, Gretchen languished at the shelter because no one wanted to pay for her $20-per-month incontinence pills. She wasn't put down because she was so sweet, but usually big, black dogs in the area don't find homes. Marie Boyum met and fell in love with her, but knew she wasn't well. Gretchen has arthritis and needs both knee and lower-spine replacements, but remains a happy girl who loves life.

gryffin
aka doodles, he is an "eternal puppy," who is always trying to get into mischief
boxer-bully mix
westminster, co
pulled from an arizona reservation by a rescue that no longer exists

Alex & Ben Tuthill (*see Ripley*) went to a small Northern Colorado rescue to see a litter of puppies that had been pulled from an Arizona reservation. They fell in love with the chunky one, Fat Albert, who was full of energy and adopted him on the spot. They changed his name to Gryffindor. He became tall and lean, shedding his former Fat Albert persona. "He brings us tremendous amounts of joy on a daily basis."

hank

aka hankers, he loves people, loves to cuddle & thinks he's a lap dog
rottweiler mix
south bend, in
pulled from northeast georgia animal shelter (negas) by saving shelter pets

Jamie Vijay (*see Lady & Penny*) adopted Hank from her rescue Saving Shelter Pets, which had pulled him from NEGAS. His entire litter had parvo, and he was the only survivor. Jamie was in charge of transporting him to Indiana and fell in love with his little puppy face immediately. He is shy around new people, but the second they look in the opposite direction, he will come up and lick their ears. "He is a great dog!"

harley

aka beastly, big bear & frank, he has his canine good citizen & loves kids & babies
catahoula leopard dog-siberian husky mix
tampa, fl
adopted from catahoula rescue inc (cri)

Kelly McDermott researched breeds and decided on a Catahoula due to their loyalty, brains and unique look. She adopted Harley after his destitute owner, who had been living in a motel, surrendered him to CRI. Amusing and handsome Harley "eats anything that does not eat him first," opens coolers to get to the ice, and ensures Kelly sees him before he grabs any "off-limits" item (a shoe, a purse, a beer...) and slinks away.

harry

aka wee-man, he is afraid of most people but is slowly learning that people are good
yorkshire terrier
fairless hills, pa
adopted from bucks county spca (bcspca); a former puppy-mill dog

Nikki & Ed Thompson adopted Harry after he was pulled from an illegal puppy mill and made available for adoption at the BCSPCA (*see pg. 149*). Scarred by his past, where he spent years caged with inadequate food and water and little to no socialization or training, he is making progress. Harry is now a BCSPCA Humane Education Dog, visiting schools and other groups to educate about the abuses that occur in puppy mills.

heartland's magnolia

aka maggie, she has her canine good citizen & is a certified therapy dog
golden retriever
auburn, me
adopted from heartland golden retriever rescue

Abuse at the second shelter she was relinquished to caused Maggie to develop many fears. Heartland was contacted to help and if they hadn't succeeded, the shelter would have put her down. Heartland placed her with Suzy & Dave Nattress, who fostered and then adopted her. Now in the right home, Maggie has blossomed. She visits the library to have kids read to her (but at times dozes off) and attends Camp Lucy each fall.

hector
proof that dogs from dog-fighting rings should be treated as individuals
american pit bull terrier
bangall, ny
adopted from bay area doglovers responsible about pitbulls (bad rap)

Hector and 48 other dogs, part of a dog-fighting ring, were pulled from NFL quarterback Michael Vick's property in 2007. Many national animal-welfare groups fought to euthanize these dogs; Best Friends Animal Society and BAD RAP fought to save them. Much to most people's surprise, Hector needed absolutely no rehabilitation. Andrew & Clara Yori adopted Hector from BAD RAP in June of 2008. The only scars from Hector's past are the ones that cover his body. Hector has no trust issues, loves people and dogs, is now a certified therapy dog, and has twice passed his Canine Good Citizen test. Hector shares his home with his athletic "brother," canine-disc champion Wallace. Although Hector is athletic, he is prevented from excelling in canine sports by his prevailing (and endearing) clumsiness. Both boys attend events to do their part to educate the public about "all dogs labeled as 'pit bulls'" and even have their own website (pitbullunited.com) and Facebook fan pages. A sweet and confident dog who loves to please, adorable Hector now lives the good life—and loves it. He shares his happy home with five other dogs, loves running around the house with a toy in his mouth, enjoys sunning himself and likes to eat his veggies (once opening a cooler to eat the carrots and not the dog treats that were inside). Hector is a bright and shining example of the resiliency of dogs.

heike
aka smiley face, she visits hospitals, hospices & nursing homes as a therapy dog
german shepherd
northern fl
adopted from big dog rescue (bdr)

Heike had been returned to her breeder and left to roam outdoors with little training or socialization. Mike & Julie Bogenreif adopted her after she licked their faces through her crate at an adoption event. Smart Heike can unlock deadbolts. The Bogenreifs got their dogs working in pet therapy after seeing Heike's sensitivity toward cancer and Alzheimer's patients. "What a wonderful, loving, compassionate dog she has become."

henry
aka beastie, he loves to follow mark around, bark at things & sleep on the couch
labrador retriever mix
afton, va
adopted from animal connections

Judy Carey Nevin & Mark Nevin had agreed that they wouldn't get a dog until Mark had finished his comprehensive exams for his PhD. Then, along came Henry who was "a neurotic mess" in need of stability. They adopted him. He had some transitioning to do, since he had never lived inside and had to learn to play. Now, the couple can't remember life pre-Henry. "We have all benefited...and we don't know what we'd do without him."

independence
aka indy, she loves sleeping on stacked dog beds like the princess & the pea
great dane
xenia, oh
adopted through 4 paws for ability (4 paws)

Karen Shirk of 4 Paws (*see Yoda*) was at the shelter the day 5-month-old Indy was brought in as a stray. Indy became a certified service dog through 4 Paws and now assists Karen, who is living with Myasthenia Gravis. Karen has been in medically controlled remission for a few years, so Indy mostly enjoys being a couch potato. She takes up the whole couch, and it takes all of Karen's kids to push her off.

itsey
loves beach walks & rolling in dead things like seals or seagulls; likes chasing squirrels
chihuahua-schipperke mix
pacific grove, ca
adopted from animal friends rescue project (afrp)

Itsey was surrendered by her owner to a local shelter. Knowing she would be hard to adopt out due to her Demodex mange problem, they called AFRP to take her. However, Itsey wasn't getting noticed in her first foster home, and so AFRP worker Karen Sheppard (*see Minnie*) decided to foster her. After four months, Karen's husband Andrew made it official, and they adopted Itsey on December 31 to celebrate the end of the year.

jaeger
this once unwanted dog "is so wanted now—we absolutely love him"
german shorthaired pointer
north wales, pa
adopted from german shorthaired pointer rescue pa

JoAnn & Rick High were looking for a friend for their active 2-year-old GSP when JoAnn, volunteering with GSP Rescue PA, saw a surrender form for a 4-year-old male. In both of Jaeger's previous homes, neither owner "had time for him." The Highs adopted him. Right away, Jaeger was a very loving dog. Since at first he didn't know how to fetch, it now makes the Highs happy to see him play. "He looks as if he's having so much fun!"

jakera
aka kera, she loves to go on rides & loves running; "jakera" means "beautiful"
catahoula leopard dog-border collie mix
nashville, tn area
adopted from c.h.a.t. adoption center of wakulla county (c.h.a.t.)

Kera was surrendered to C.H.A.T. by her owner for unknown reasons. Sue W. (*see Tye*) was looking for a pal for her dog Tye when she found beautiful Kera on Petfinder and knew she was hers; she had the eyes of Sue's old dog Jake. Kera and Tye are now great friends, loving to wrestle and play. Kera has a way of asking Sue for things; she puts her foot on the item she wants and looks up at Sue for her permission to have it.

jasper
just wants to hug & lick everyone; he loves to wrestle & play tug with "brother" bailey
australian shepherd
crofton, md
adopted from aussie rescue & placement helpline (arph)

Jasper was surrendered to ARPH when he was 18 months old after his owner became too ill to care for him. Debbie & Michael Brown quickly adopted this beautiful boy, who now shares his home with agility Aussie Bailey. Jasper, however, is a rare "couch potato" Aussie. When Debbie introduced him to agility, he promptly entered a tunnel and went to sleep. "He clearly thinks a rescued dog should not have to work for his dinner."

jeep
loves people & kids; "his tail wags so much you can almost hear it"
american pit bull terrier-labrador retriever mix
shillington, pa
adopted from second time around rescue (star)

Jules Stoud (*see Wrangler*) was volunteering for STAR when she was asked to transport two dogs to the rescue. They had been pulled from a West Virginia shelter, where their time was running out. Jeep, who was so dirty his brown coat looked black, started wagging his tail as soon as he saw Jules, and she knew right then he was hers. Jeep thinks he is a lap dog. He loves swimming and jumping up and down like a kangaroo.

jesse james
"jesse wakes me every morning with a toy in his mouth & a sparkle in his eye"
collie
woodland hills, ca
adopted from southland collie rescue (scr)

A family relinquished 10-month-old wild Jesse claiming they could no longer care for him. Confined to a crate all his young life, he was obese, had matted fur and weak and bent hind legs from lack of use. He knew no commands. After Karen & Ken Laramay (*see Samantha & Sundance Kid*) adopted him, Jesse blossomed into "the most endearing and loving collie I have ever known!" Now trained and healthy, he competes in agility.

jessie
loves kids & works with them at a school for the autistic & through paws for reading
american pit bull terrier-labrador retriever mix
locust grove, va
adopted from her previous owner

After a few failed adoptions, Jessie was fostered by Samantha Duvall, who was then living with her parents. She wanted to adopt her, but her parents weren't so sure. On her birthday, they at last told her that Jessie was hers to keep. "She is the BEST birthday gift I've ever received!" Jessie is now a certified Pet Partner, has her Canine Good Citizen, competes in rally-o and has completed Animal Assisted Crisis Response Training.

johann
aka yoyo, he knows 30+ commands & holds too many titles & certifications to name
shetland sheepdog
dayton, tn
adopted from southside animal shelter (ssas)

Leslie May adopted Johann when he was 12 weeks old from no-kill shelter SSAS. Johann has since become a star agility dog, and a bit of a celebrity with his own website (johannthedog.com), Twitter account and Facebook fan page. Leslie, Johann, Border Collie "sister" Gracie and two cats, now live in a cabin in the lovely Tennessee mountains surrounded by 100 acres, where YoYo enjoys hiking and learning new tricks.

katie
loves dogs, loves attention & loves people; she will lick the face of anyone she meets
great dane
belfast, me
adopted from her original owner

Maggie Smith (*see Rufus*) adopted stunning blue-merle Katie from a private owner when Katie was just 4 months old. She fit right in with the three male Danes Maggie had at the time—so much so that Maggie quickly referred to Katie as one of the boys. Sadly, two of her "brothers" have since passed, but two new Danes have joined the pack. Gentle Katie loves people; if you are sitting, this 135-lb. lap dog will back right up and sit in your lap.

lacy hannah
aka lacy, she loves to play with socks, both on feet & off
chihuahua-maltese mix
alexandria, va
rescued from a puppy mill

A vet in Kentucky had taken in dogs from a puppy-mill bust. Lacy was one of them. The vet's Virginia-based son was helping to rehome the dogs. Michelle D'Ettorre (*see Remy Martin*) saw the ad online and adopted Lacy. Cute Lacy loves to take stuffed animals, toss them in the air, chase them down, and do it all over again. Every night, Lacy crawls into bed and, through a series of whiny half-barks, will "tell [Michelle] about her day."

lady (bond)
aka lay-lay, sweetie pie & miss piggy, she loves to eat
rhodesian ridgeback-labrador retriever mix
baltimore, md
adopted from partnership for animal welfare (p.a.w.s.)

When June & Terry Bond (*see Ce-Ce & Chloe*) adopted Lady from P.A.W.S. it was love at first sight. She is truly a lady. Lady is extremely friendly and loves people and snuggling. She loves to lie in the sun, get belly rubs, go on walks and car rides, and take trips in the motorhome, but she hates the rain. She is certified with Pets on Wheels to visit the elderly. Lady will stare at the treat jar pathetically until she gets a treat.

lady (mcnamara-miller)
loves the water & especially loves swimming in the pond on her property
american staffordshire terrier
sioux falls, sd
adopted from pit rescue of the great plains (prgp)

Clint Miller, Jennifer McNamara & daughter Casey Miller (*see Ginger*) share their lives with Lady. Lady was at PRGP for just over a year when they adopted her. She had come to the rescue as a young puppy after she was found abandoned in a ditch outside town. "Our dogs live a great life!" The girls, Lady and Ginger, now have a third dog, a 3-year-old miniature poodle adopted in 2009, to keep them in line.

lady (vijay)
initially afraid of everyone, lady showed only love for an autistic boy jamie worked with
english (redtick) coonhound
south bend, in
adopted from mixed up mutts (mum)

Jamie Vijay (*see Hank & Penny*) spotted skinny Lady up for adoption at PetSmart. "There was something in her that seemed so sad. I adopted her that day." Relinquished by a breeder, Lady had been kept for years in an outdoor cage so small that her paws didn't form properly. She wasn't socialized, couldn't walk right and was fearful. Over the last seven years, she has become "a real dog," is less afraid and now loves new people.

lil' britches
aka little man & little b, he loved chasing his new dog friends around the shop
miniature pinscher
san clemente, ca
adopted from a small, local rescue

Kristen (*see Angus & Sampson*) was looking for a small dog on Petfinder when she saw a photo of an old min pin with bulgy eyes that said, "I'm the one." He had been at a rescue for two years after his owner died. Social Britches bonded with his new "brothers" instantly and spent every day at Kristen's shop with his many new friends, including kids who spoiled him. He recently passed away and will be missed by all who knew him.

lucie
aka ma'am, lucifer & bear, she loves flyball, agility & wrestling with "brother" zip
labrador retriever-boxer mix
lizella, ga
found dumped along the side of the road

Sue & Nate Painter-Thorne (*see Pezziwig & Zip*) couldn't catch Lucie (short for "elusive") when they first saw her run into the road, trying to escape from an armadillo. They needed to return the next day with a crate and some food in order to catch her. She was 8 months old, emaciated and covered with ticks. "Considering her start in life, she has an amazing temperament. She is a very sweet, attentive, playful and smart dog."

lucy
aka lucy-goose, loves to chase balls, squirrels, rabbits (you name it) & loves to swim
german shepherd-australian cattle dog mix
estes park, co
adopted from humane society of boulder valley (hsbv)

When Emily Gubler got Lucy from the HSBV, Lucy's femur was smashed, probably by a car. The smashed bone was removed, and she now has a "false joint" (her leg is held on by muscle), but she copes well. Lucy loves everyone, and when she meets new people she wiggles her whole back end. Lucy has learned hand signals from watching her deaf "sister" Roxy and responds even better to signs than she does to verbal commands.

lydia lamb
aka lydia; loves sunning herself & distracting "brother" archie in order to steal his snack
australian shepherd-border collie mix
austin, tx
adopted from town lake animal center (austin's animal control)

The whole household was grieving over the loss of their dog Lucy when Therese Kopiwoda (*see Archibald Bo MacLeod*) decided to adopt another dog. The minute Lydia walked into the house, everyone perked up. "We were meant to be together!" Lydia has hip dysplasia, but altering her diet has helped her mobility. Diagnosed with cancer in 2008, she endured 9 months of chemotherapy and has been in remission ever since.

mabel (bennett-mitchell)
speed-demon mabel uses her large yard as her own personal racetrack
golden retriever-shar pei mix
batesville, va
adopted from animal connections

Mabel, found as a stray in Northern Virginia and placed in a high-kill shelter, was rescued by Animal Connections. Arin Bennett & Ashley Mitchell (*see Eva & Monty*) were looking for a pal for their dog Eva when they heard about Mabel. Eva and Mabel became instant playmates, and Mabel has been a family member ever since. Mabel always has a stick in her mouth. She insists on daily belly rubs and loves to chase and be chased.

mabel (wiberg)
mabel is "nothing but love with a tail;" she "makes the grouchiest people smile"
basset hound
san clemente, ca
rescued off the streets of puerto rico

Roger C. Wiberg II's friend Denise Swift (*see Francisco, Twinkie & Wilfredo*) found Mabel dying in a pool of blood on the roadside after a hit and run. She had a fractured skull, jaw and hip, internal injuries and her eyeballs were dislodged. While healing, she escaped and got hit again, hence the nickname "Speed Bump." Roger adopted her and said, "She's the best dog I've ever had—the bond was instant, companions for life."

madonna

many of her own puppies will be service dogs; the orphaned litter is up for adoption
golden retriever-labrador retriever mix
xenia, oh
in training at 4 paws for ability (4 paws)

A family found Madonna on their front porch on Christmas day. They brought her inside, where, much to the family's surprise, Madonna gave birth to five puppies. All of the dogs were adopted by 4 Paws. Five weeks later, an orphaned litter of puppies appeared. Long story short, loving Madonna was a great mom to both her litter and the new litter—16 puppies in total! She is now in service-dog training to work with a disabled child.

martin

aka mr. paddles (due to his paddle feet & great swimming ability); he's a pro snuggler
dachshund (he is a tweenie, not a standard & not a miniature, but in-between)
austin, tx
adopted from central texas dachshund rescue (ctdr)

Forced by the town to relinquish some of their many dogs, Martin's owners surrendered "the old one" (he was 6) to CTDR. Martin then became the failed foster of Sue Rostvold & Allan Little. They discovered his severe heart murmur months later. He is now on medication, and has had several close calls, but remains loving, happy and active. Martin is an avid swimmer, performs swan dives and does the "chicken dance" for food.

maude

a real character who loves to track & loves to drool; "spit flinging" is her only sport
bloodhound
the wilds of alaska
adopted from 4 paws for ability (4 paws)

With sore marks and scars on her face, infected ears and wrinkles and a thin body, Maude was an unlikely candidate for assistance-dog training. However, 4 Paws chose her, and she passed all of her temperament tests. Maude, however, failed their Autism Assistance Dog program and was put up for adoption by 4 Paws. Now healthy and happy, loving Maude has a great home with a family that has bloodhound experience.

max

aka sonny, king sun, bubba, mashed potatohead, moshki, bobo & the great white hope
akita or akita mix
san clemente, ca
found as a stray

Found on the streets of LA's Chinatown by Denise Swift (*see Francisco, Twinkie & Wilfredo*), Max was just a dirty gray fluffball of a puppy. Denise's sister Cory Swift & Neil Russell (*see Cici & Vanna*) took him in, even though their landlord didn't allow pets. Max, still going strong at 13, is the certified "King of Cool." He seems to know what you are going to say before you say it. "There is just something really special about Max."

memphis

amanda often took kind, loving memphis to school with her when she was a teacher
american pit bull terrier mix
hobbs, nm
adopted from a high-kill shelter where only 10 percent of the dogs make it out alive

Weston, Amanda & Savannah Green (*see Shania & Uno*) adopted Memphis from Hobbs Animal Shelter, after Amanda heard him "yapping his head off" while she was handing out treats to the dogs ("my philosophy was to at least let them meet a kind hand before being euthanized"). He was a bloody mess whose ears had just been cropped; his days were numbered. They planned to foster him, but talkative Memphis was home to stay.

mimi

a stubborn "tomboy," who prefers to play rough with the big dogs
beagle mix
atlanta, ga
adopted from deaf paws haven

Mimi was surrendered to a kill shelter by her previous owner because he didn't have time to train her. Due to be put down at any moment, Mimi was pulled and fostered by Cathy Miller through her rescue Deaf Paws Haven. On Day 3 of fostering, Mimi chewed up a wooden chair. Cathy knew sturdier toys and increased exercise time were needed. That fixed everything, and Mimi's foster home soon became her forever home.

minnie

"such a sweet, loving dog" who loves kids & loves going for walks
chihuahua
pacific grove, ca
adopted from animal friends rescue project (afrp)

Karen & Andrew Sheppard (*see Itsey*) adopted Minnie from AFRP when she was about 8 years old. AFRP got her from the city shelter in Salinas, which had picked her up as a stray. The vet, who suspected Minnie had had many litters, removed a few mammary tumors from her, pulled many of her teeth and had her spayed. Now happy and healthy, she loves being outside on a sunny day, stretched out to catch every single sunbeam.

miracle houdini

aka miracle, mira & honey, she loves to look out the window & watch the world go by
akita-chow chow mix
otego, ny
found along the side of the road

Found as a stray, emaciated and infested with worms, 2-month-old Miracle was left for dead along the roadside. Mary Ellen Mack saw her on Petfinder and adopted her. Named "Miracle" for beating the odds, she has hip dysplasia and bad knees, likely caused by early malnutrition. She got called "Houdini" after, on three separate occasions, she escaped from three different crates, all with three different types of latches.

monty
an intense starer, he is always active, loving to play tag, wrestle & chase tennis balls
hound mix
batesville, va
adopted from saving furry friends

Found as a stray (probably an abandoned hunting dog), Monty was placed in a high-kill shelter in southwest Virginia and was due to be euthanized within hours. Saving Furry Friends posted Monty's photo on Facebook and Arin Bennett & Ashley Mitchell (*see Eva & Mabel*), after seeing his sad and sullen eyes, agreed to take him. Monty is now a happy-go-lucky dog. He loves to cuddle next to, and on top of, his "siblings."

mudd puppy
a lovebug who would rather be with his family than anywhere else
catahoula leopard dog
grandview, tn
adopted from catahoula united rescue society (c.u.r.s.)

Stunning Mudd Puppy was born, along with his seven littermates, in a high-kill Georgia shelter where his mother had been brought in as a stray. Luckily, C.U.R.S. pulled and fostered them, and Mudd Puppy soon got a great home with Scott & Joanna Ray, who foster Catahoulas. He is now surrounded by a loving family and acres of land to play on with his many dog "siblings." "We are so lucky to have such a loving and caring dog!"

murphy
aka mooshy & smurfy, he loves flyball, car rides, bones & tennis balls
hound mix
baltimore, md
born in a foster home after his mother was pulled from a kill shelter

The day before she was due to be put down, Murphy's mother was pulled from a West Virginia shelter by a rescue that didn't know she was pregnant. Murphy was born in one of the rescue's foster homes. Jennifer Strong (*see Nittany*) found Murphy on Petfinder. Shy but loving, Murphy adores his "sister" Nittany and the home's cats. One cat steals food from his dish, and patient and tolerant Murphy just waits for her to finish.

natasha
a certified canine good citizen & therapy dog, she is getting disaster dog certification
american staghound
palmyra, pa
adopted from helping hands pet rescue (helping hands)

Lisa Hetzel & John Claeys adopted beautiful Natasha from Helping Hands after seeing her on Petfinder. Natasha was pulled from a Florida breeder who had become overwhelmed with dogs; the dogs had been confined to pens with little human contact. Lisa & John drove to the Gainesville, Florida area to pick her up. Today, Natasha shares her home with five other dogs and three cats. She competes in freestyle and agility.

nicholas ivan
aka nick, he has his canine good citizen & is a certified therapy dog
border collie mix
rogers, ar
adopted from humane society for animals

Steve, Toni & Georgia Carter adopted Nick from the Humane Society for Animals where Steve & Toni both volunteer. Having walked Nick every Saturday for six months, Steve couldn't bear to bring Nick back to the shelter after he failed to get noticed at an adoption event. Instead, Steve brought him home. "Welcoming ambassador" at the dog park, Nick loves rolling in anything stinky. He is "calm, attentive, insanely kind" and much loved.

nittany
aka nit-wit & fuzz face, she participates in agility & flyball & is a certified therapy dog
golden retriever-husky-chow chow mix
baltimore, md
adopted from animal protection alliance (apa)

Nittany was found chained outside with a 3-foot lead and a tight collar around her neck. Her owners had always kept her outside "because she shed." APA got them to relinquish her. Soon afterward, Jennifer Strong (*see Murphy*) adopted her. Nittany loves kids and is very gentle with them. She adores everyone and will forgo food if she thinks there is a chance someone in the room will pet her.

penny
aka penny poo, now in her golden years, she still loves to run & play in the backyard
beagle-american pit bull terrier mix
south bend, in
adopted from humane society of st. joseph county (hssjc) (now a no-kill facility)

Jamie Vijay (*see Hank & Lady*) and her family adopted Penny from HSSJC on the day Penny was due to be put down. Penny and 12-year-old Jamie bonded instantly and have been inseparable ever since. Penny is still very active. Loyal and obedient from the start, she is very smart; this old dog can and does learn new tricks. "She has been my best friend for the last 18 years...she's the sweetest dog anyone could ever hope for."

pezziwig
aka pezz, pezzi, wiggle & little bit, she chases tennis balls relentlessly & loves flyball
border collie
lizella, ga
found dumped along the side of the road

Pezziwig was found dumped on a backroad at 8 months old. She had fly bites and calluses and was unsocialized and untrained. Because of their prior experience with Border Collies, Sue & Nate Painter-Thorne (*see Lucie & Zip*) were asked to help modify some OCD behavior Pezz was exhibiting. They took her home to foster, and there she stayed. She loves cuddling, playing keep-away with "sister" Zoom and playing tug.

phoenix

she has her canine good citizen, is a certified pet partner & knows 30+ commands
border collie
stafford, va
adopted from local animal control

Phoenix was filthy when Jackie Pratt first saw her at the shelter, but Jackie couldn't resist her sweet face. Smart Phoenix is a real character. She will bring you a toy when you are busy, and if you don't want to play with that one, she'll bring you another, and another, until she has emptied the toy bin. She will also unravel the toilet paper roll by pulling on the end and backing out of the room. She competes in obedience and rally-o.

porter

a certified canine good citizen & therapy dog, he is also an expert door & latch opener
pitador retrievabull (american pit bull terrier-labrador retriever mix)
pittsburgh, pa
adopted from western pennsylvania humane society (wphs)

Traveling often for work, Porter's previous owner kept him confined in the basement for days while he was away. Untrained and probably never walked, Porter was 2.5 years old when Amy Dengler (*see Dena*) adopted him from WPHS. Since then he has blossomed, even starring in a nationwide anti dog-fighting public service announcement. Porter is now a demo dog in the Pit Bull Ambassador class that Amy teaches locally.

remy martin

aka remy, he is a certified therapy dog & works at a library where kids read to him
chihuahua-pomeranian mix
alexandria, va
adopted from his previous owner

A shelter worker adopted out a spayed Chihuahua female to a family with a neutered male Chihuahua. Turns out neither dog was fixed (and one or both weren't purebreds). Remy and his littermates were the result. Michelle D'Ettorre (*see Lacy Hannah*) adopted him after seeing an ad online. Remy loves throwing balls down the steps, retrieving them and repeating. An avid sunbather, Remy, on walks, will stop and smell the flowers.

ripley (long ayscue)

aka rip, ripple dipple & hound dog, he is a marathon digger & counter surfer
basset hound-dachshund mix
hertford, nc
adopted from spca of northeastern north carolina (spca of nenc)

After a breeder let her dachshund run lose and get impregnated by the neighbor's basset, she surrendered the litter to the SPCA. Ripley, adopted out three times, was ill and neglected at his third home. Holly Long Ayscue (*see Ziggy*) stepped in and adopted him. Food crazy Ripley counter surfs to find every last crumb he can. He copes fine with his two club feet, and his looks attract attention, which he readily eats up, too!

ripley (tuthill)

aka mooshu; will gently pull you outside to play; loves to sit as close to you as she can
american pit bull terrier mix
westminster, co
adopted from humane society of boulder valley (hsbv)

Ripley and her littermates were transferred from a Denver shelter, due to the city's breed-specific ban, to the HSBV, where Alex & Ben Tuthill (*see Gryffin*) volunteer. Alex fell in love with Ripley and planned on adopting her on her birthday. However, the night before her birthday, someone broke into the shelter and stole the puppies. Ripley was found the following day, and they quickly adopted her. Ripley hasn't left their sight since.

rocky

he loves to sniff out discarded chicken bones on walks & to bay at unsuspecting dogs
beagle-basset hound mix
philadelphia, pa
adopted from animal welfare association (awa)

Knowing elderly dogs have a hard time getting adopted, Catherine & Charles Rombeau (*see Franklin*) adopted "10-year-old" Rocky from AWA after seeing him on Petfinder. Their vet, however, downgraded this senior's age to a more middle-aged 7. Rocky has a benign tumor, has lost teeth due to poor care early in life and has an endearing slope, of unknown origin, to his head, but all else about him is healthy, especially his appetite.

roxy

"an attention hog;" obedience-class star-pupil roxy does 360-degree spins for treats
basenji mix
conshohocken, pa
adopted from philadelphia animal welfare society (paws) adoption event

Jana Landon & Gerry Pasquarello share their lives with Roxy, who was adopted after Jana met Roxy at an adoption event and fell in love with how friendly, loving and outgoing she was. Roxy had just had a litter of puppies and was so skinny "you could count her ribs from across the room." Always happy, always energetic, playful Roxy wags her tail with her entire body, is one fast running partner and is always eager to please.

rufus

he "loved, loved, loved everybody," was great with kids & the home's many foster dogs
great dane
belfast, me
adopted from "a seriously irresponsible owner"

When Maggie Smith (*see Katie*) adopted Rufus, her first Dane, from his previous owner, 1-year-old Rufus was not housebroken, could not walk on leash, knew no manners and was scared. Maggie turned things around. Rufus made Maggie fall in love with the breed and was her entrance into Dane rescue. Sadly, he fell ill and passed away in the fall of 2009. "A true ambassador for the breed," he is missed terribly by those who knew him.

sadie

thousands of deaf dogs are put down each year; sadie was one of the lucky ones
bordador (border collie-labrador retriever mix)
philadelphia, pa
adopted from bucks county spca (bcspca)

Sadie's mother passed on her deafness to her whole litter. Realizing the pups were deaf, the owner relinquished them to the BCSPCA. Melissa McDaniel adopted her after visiting the shelter with her nephews. "Having a deaf dog is like having any other dog. I just use hand signals instead of verbal commands." Sadie loves chasing butterflies and bugs. Loved beyond words, Sadie was the inspiration for the photo book projects.

samantha

aka sammysam; bred for 10 years during which she endured severe cruelty & neglect
collie
woodland hills, ca
adopted from southland collie rescue (scr)

A woman called SCR after seeing Samantha covered in feces, foxtails and filth in a nearby yard. Sam's gums were shredded to the jawbone where she had been chewing on rocks. She was fearful and extremely submissive. The vet repaired her gums with skin grafts and pulled eight teeth. Karen & Ken Laramay (*see Jesse James & Sundance Kid*) intended to foster her, but couldn't let this sweet girl go. She had won their hearts.

sampson

aka sampsonwampson, he loves to swim & chase his "brother" in & out of waves
american pit bull terrier
san clemente, ca
adopted from canine crusaders

Sampson, originally rescued from a bad home in Los Angeles, had two or three homes before finding Kristen (*see Angus & Lil' Britches*). He managed to run away from each, but once Kristen adopted him, he never ran away again, even when a gate, accidentally left open, gave him the chance. Sampson, hoping for a ride, will sit in Kristen's parked car for hours. Sampson is an active 11 year old, enjoying long hikes and camping.

sawyer

aka soybean & beanie, he's a service dog (mobility), therapy dog & flyball champion
australian shepherd
sykesville, md
found on the australian shepherd rescue page (asrp)

Erin Saywell added Sawyer, who had been found as a stray in Missouri, to her pack after she saw him on ASRP. Soon afterward they met John Deitrich, who was looking for a new service dog. Erin joked that he should use Sawyer, and John took her seriously. The job fit Sawyer like a glove; he seemed to know his role from the start. He can help John undress, pick up items that he drops and fetch things that he wants or needs.

shania

loves to sunbathe, chase rabbits & cuddle, she opened the greens' minds to "pit bulls"
american pit bull terrier
hobbs, nm
abandoned at a veterinary clinic's boarding facility

Weston, Amanda & Savannah Green (*see Memphis & Uno*) live with Shania. Shania's owners brought her in to a vet's office to board and never returned for her. The vet had no luck rehoming this pit bull until Amanda, who was working at the vet, brought her home for Christmas and kept her. Amanda never really understood people's attachment to their pets, but understands now "thanks to the love and devotion Shania and I share."

stevie

loves kids; visits schools & other organizations as a bcspca humane education dog
corgi-beagle-terrier mix
morrisville, pa
adopted from bucks county spca (bcspca)

Brought in to the BCSPCA as a stray, Stevie was adopted by John, Debbie, Amanda & John M. Dubell (*see Bella Bean*). She was thin, one of her eyes was twice the size of the other and she had Lyme disease. Smart Stevie is blind in both eyes, but that doesn't keep her from doing anything that she wants to do, such as playing fetch, swimming and wrestling with "sister" Bella. "She finds new ways to amaze us each and every day!"

sundance kid

with training & love, he became a champion agility & therapy dog; he loves to please
collie
woodland hills, ca
adopted from southland collie rescue (scr)

Stunning Sundance had been placed in seven homes before he was found wandering the countryside and picked up by SCR's Regional Coordinator Karen Laramay (*see Jesse James & Samantha*). He was skinny, blind in one eye, had been debarked and was desperate for love. Karen & her husband Ken knew he was special and adopted him. He didn't wag his tail for a year. When at last he did, it was "a celebration for all."

sunny

aka ms. sunny ("nunny" is what their 18-month-old daughter christine calls her)
american pit bull terrier
indianapolis, in
adopted from dogs deserve better (ddb)

Found outside of an office with a broken leg—presumably from a hit and run—in Hobbs, New Mexico, Sunny was rescued by DDB who paid for her necessary leg amputation due to injuries sustained in the accident. She was adopted by Christel & Jessee Uhde, who saw her on Petfinder, and fell in love. Showing no signs she knows she is missing a leg, Sunny loves to dig huge holes in the backyard and chase squirrels.

taffy

aka li'l bit & sweetpea; taffy loves to eat & does her very own taffy treat dance
miniature rat terrier
elizabethtown, nc
adopted from ratbone rescues; a former puppy-mill breeder dog

From her ex-life as a puppy-mill breeder dog, Taffy has deformed hips and rear legs from being constantly bred and from life in a wire-floor cage (she has since developed arthritis in these joints), and needed to have seven teeth pulled due to severe periodontal disease. When she was no longer able to have as many puppies as was deemed profitable, she was placed in a high-kill shelter, but saved by Ratbone Rescues and Cheryl L Willoughby adopted her. "Something about her face tugged at my heartstrings. When I learned her story, I knew she needed to come live with my mom and me." Having only lived in an outdoor cage, Taffy needed to adjust to life in a home. She was fearful of strangers at first, but has since learned that people are fun. She also had to learn to play, and to play with toys. She adapted to home life quickly and now when people meet her they don't believe she ever lived in a puppy mill—the only proof is the tattoos in her ears, which were the breeder's identification marks. Taffy is a sock thief, who likes to "collect" people's socks and hoard them. She loves squeaky toys and getting belly rubs. Cheryl's mother is legally blind, and Taffy has taken on the role of being her personal guard and caretaker. When Cheryl leaves the house, she tells Taffy to "take care of GrandMargie," and adorable Taffy immediately jumps in her mom's lap. She is her "special eye dog."

toby

loves people, he can follow a series of commands in order & is skilled at opening doors
australian shepherd mix
lansdale, pa
adopted from a small local rescue that no longer exists

Found as a stray and placed in a high-kill shelter in Kentucky, Toby was pulled by a small Pennsylvania rescue. Allison & Mike Fanelli (*see Tucker*) had just lost their dog, and surfing Petfinder one day Allison came across an endearing letter written "by Toby" and fell in love. He became her "best birthday present ever!" Toby hoards objects like sticks, bones, and toys and stores them in his little dog "cave" under an endtable.

tucker (bartlett-sullivan)

a very spoiled "comfort creature—always looking for the cushiest spot to nap in"
american pit bull terrier-pointer mix
baltimore, md
adopted from baltimore animal rescue & care shelter (barcs); ethical bull breed rescue & referral (ebbrr)

Tucker and his littermates were going to be put down if a rescue couldn't help. At that time, BARCS did not adopt out any pit bulls (but are very pit-bull friendly today). Erin Sullivan & Rob Bartlett (*see Doc*) adopted Tucker after Erin, who was at the shelter evaluating a dog for EBBRR, took him to foster. Lovable Tucker is "kind of like one giant quirky, funny, odd personality trait...He's been the perfect dog for us in every way."

tucker (fanelli)

loves messy beds—as soon as the fanellis make the bed, tucker goes & "unmakes" it
labrador retriever mix
lansdale, pa
adopted from montgomery county spca (mcspca)

Allison & Mike Fanelli (*see Toby*) went to the MCSPCA with their daughter and heard over the intercom: "incoming puppy." They raced to the lobby to see cute Tucker being turned in by a truck driver who didn't have time for him. They adopted Tucker. It took a while for him to warm up to people, but he is now making up for lost time: this 60-lb. lap dog loves to cuddle and will sit on the lap of anyone who is on the couch.

twinkie

aka li'l mama, she is the "sweetest, most obedient little fluff of tough cuteness"
shih tzu mix
monterey, ca
rescued from a backyard breeder in puerto rico

Denise Swift (*see Francisco & Wilfredo*) heard from her vet about a sick puppy that he had rescued from a backyard breeder. The breeder had been hoping to get a certificate of good health from the vet in order to sell the dog to a pet store. Twinkie, who has severe allergies, was near death, with ear and eye infections, extreme pyoderma and immune system failure. She was hospitalized for a week before Denise could adopt her.

tye

aka beau tye, he has his canine good citizen & is a very outgoing boy
border collie
nashville, tn area
adopted from humane society of elmore county (hsec)

Sue W. (*see Jakera*) was looking on Petfinder after losing her much loved dog Jake. She found "spunky" Tye at HSEC and drove to Alabama to see him. Tye was smart, tough, stubborn with a sense of humor and a constant smile, and was just the dog Sue needed. On December 10, 2007, Tye found his forever home. He knows many commands and can do an "upside down smile"—he rolls over on his back and shows his teeth.

uno

aka uney bambooney & the big white hype; a momma's boy who loves little savannah
american pit bull terrier-dogo argentino-american bulldog mix
hobbs, nm
born in a foster home that became his forever home

Weston, Amanda & Savannah Green (*see Memphis & Shania*) rescued Uno's mom after answering the ad "Free red nose pit bull to good home" in a local paper. His mom weighed half her ideal weight, and while at the Greens', she gave birth to Uno, the only pup in the litter. Uno has his Canine Good Citizen, and since he was 1 year old he has visited nursing homes, schools and troubled youth homes as a certified therapy dog.

vanna

aka vanna bean, beanie, string bean, house mouse, peppa, baby & schubert
chihuahua mix
san clemente, ca
found as a stray in canovanas (from which she gets her name), puerto rico

Denise Swift (*see Francisco, Twinkie & Wilfredo*) found skinny 6-month-old Vanna along the roadside. After being treated for a blood disease, she was flown to California to live with Cory Swift & Neil Russell (*see Cici & Max*). Vanna is a certified princess, is well-adjusted, shows no scars from her old street life and is a true athlete. If you say "racetrack," she "ignites into a white furball of fire" zipping around at full speed.

wilfredo

aka woof, he is a "control freak"
terrier-chow chow mix
monterey, ca
found as a stray in puerto rico

Wilfredo was an "abused, neurotic, shaggy mess" when Denise Swift (*see Francisco*) found him while she was hiking though the rain forest in Puerto Rico. He quickly bonded with Denise and stole her heart. He is the dog that inspired her to start her rescue work in Puerto Rico, which resulted in her saving the lives of countless street dogs (*see Cici, Frankie, Mabel, Twinkie & Vanna*). Wilfredo is a therapy dog.

willow

loves being outside in the snow in wintertime & going for a swim in summertime
german shepherd-husky mix
severna park, md
adopted from maryland spca (baltimore)

Phyllis & Mark Hayden (*see Zipping thru the Darkside*) adopted Willow from the Maryland SPCA when she was just 8 weeks old (and unbelievably cute). Their kids were so excited when they came home from school that day and saw this adorable puppy. Six months earlier, the Haydens had lost their old dog. "It was really nice to have some joy in our house again." Now 12 years old, Willow was a star agility dog in her younger years.

winnie

a certified house hearing dog, she is trained to assist the deaf & hard of hearing
chihuahua mix
norristown, pa
adopted through dogs for the deaf (dfd); pulled from central california spca (ccspca)

Donna, who began losing her hearing later in life, adopted Winnie through DFD, a non-profit that pulls shelter dogs and trains them to be hearing dogs. (Winnie had been picked up as a stray by CCSPCA.) Winnie alerts Donna whenever she hears the doorbell, smoke detector, telephone, tea kettle, stove timer or other timer. She loves to eat, chase squirrels and hide under blankets. "Winnie is my helper, my companion and my joy."

woodrow

aka woody; bird watcher & squirrel hater; knows the word "groceries" means mealtime
basset hound
tallahassee, fl
adopted from panhandle animal welfare society (paws)

Probably abandoned for failing at hunting, Woody was found wandering a highway near Crestview, Florida. He was emaciated, infested with fleas and had eye and respiratory infections. Steve & Valerie Gardner's daughter saw him online and visited him at PAWS. The Gardners adopted him the next day. Woody is a character. When he is in trouble, he pretends he is asleep, and when he is hot, he sticks his nose in his water bowl.

wrangler

true to his name, he loves going off-roading (but hates the mud)
american pit bull terrier-beagle mix
shillington, pa
adopted from second time around rescue (star)

Jules Stoud (*see Jeep*) went to STAR to see a young puppy who had been transported up from North Carolina. When she saw this adorable "poof of fur" running towards her, her heart stopped. She adopted him that day. Wrangler enjoys wrestling with his "brother" Jeep, ripping stuffed toys to shreds, playing with tennis balls and "playing soccer." He and his brother are "spoiled rotten."

yoda

as 4 paws ambassador, he gets fan mail from kids all over the world
papillon mix
xenia, oh
adopted from animal friends humane society; works for 4 paws for ability (4 paws)

5-year-old Yoda jumped into the arms of Karen Shirk of 4 Paws (*see Independence*) while she was at Animal Friends to get a 4 Paws dog. Yoda wasn't service-dog material, but she knew she could rehome him. However, he fit right in to her home and there he stayed. "Yoda is ambassador for 4 Paws. He helps the other Papillons run 4pawsdogs. org, has a web page on the site and tells the kids who their new service dogs will be."

zeke

aka zekers & ezekial, he has his own couch & loves to spend his days napping on it
great dane
fargo, nd
surrendered to bentley's buds great dane rescue (bbgdr)

Purchased originally from a backyard breeder, Zeke was relinquished to Nykky Rehovsky's rescue BBGDR by his owner, who had 30 Miniature Pinschers, and who abused Zeke and left him crated most of the day. Zeke was 8 months old and underweight, but was happy at last to be loved. Zeke adopted Nykky. He bonded with her and had no desire to adapt to other potential homes—so, with Nykky he stayed.

ziggy
aka "the fun police," because when the other pets are playing, he'll bark until they stop
american eskimo dog or pomeranian mix
hertford, nc
adopted from his previous owner

Ziggy was passed from home to home: an elderly woman who died; then that woman's son; then the son's handyman; and finally the handyman's neighbor (the handyman went on vacation, left Ziggy with a neighbor and never returned to retrieve him). Holly Long Ayscue (*see Ripley*) heard about Ziggy and adopted him. Smart Ziggy knows many commands, including one to bark at the cat to get the cat to stop clawing the furniture.

zip
a "nanny" to the other dogs; knows when "brother" oliver is about to have a seizure
rat terrier
lizella, ga
adopted from all about animals (aaa)

When Sue & Nate Painter-Thorne (*see Lucie & Pezziwig*) adopted Zip, he had Demodex mange and almost no fur, was skinny and lacked muscle tone; he had been surrendered to AAA in this state. Now happy and healthy, Zip loves new people so much he will jump into a stranger's lap uninvited. Completely fearless, an amazing athlete and a champion flyballer, Zip loves to chase squirrels and birds and will even climb trees to get to them.

zipping thru the darkside
aka zipper, he competes in agility, has herded sheep & likes to do just about anything
border collie
severna park, md
adopted from howard county animal control & adoption center

Phyllis & Mark Hayden (*see Willow*) weren't looking for another dog when a friend, the director of local animal control, told them about Zipper. They met him and soon took him home. If it moves, Zipper wants to herd it; he'll herd vacuums, brooms, rakes and trash cans if you are bringing them in from the street. A born comedian, Zipper submerges his head to blow bubbles in the pool, and likes to play with feet and remove socks.

bella bean, daisy, darcy & harry
a humane society police officer's account of a 2009 puppy-mill raid
yorkshire terriers
bucks county, pa
bucks county spca

"I am a Humane Society Police Officer with Bucks County SPCA. On Saturday, March 28th, 2009 at 2 am, I received a phone call from Upper Makefield Police that they had found a situation with many dogs in an abandoned home. Shelter employee Megan Costello, Executive Director, Anne Irwin, and I showed up to the home by 2:25 am, where we found the 46 dogs living in deplorable conditions. There were 22 cages, most containing multiple dogs, that were filthy with urine and fecal matter, matted hair, and other physical issues. By 6 am, Officer Harry Vitello of Upper Makefield Police Department and I had written a search warrant, had it signed by a judge and were ready to serve it at 7 am. Anne and Megan readied the vehicles with cages and equipment to transfer the dogs back to our shelter. The Upper Makefield Police and Bucks County SPCA staff worked to identify and remove all of the dogs. By 8 am, all of the dogs were back at our shelter where they were photographed and examined for physical conditions. Harry was found in Cage 13, with a large female Yorkie later to be named Darcy. (Darcy, as well as most of the other females, were bred over and over again. Some of them had their uteruses fall apart when they were spayed. Some also had multiple Cesarean section scars. I believe that they were bred at each available heat, and not given any break between litters.) Harry was assigned the number "13a" and Darcy became "13b." There were five male Yorkies that did not have names, and since there were five officers helping to remove the dogs, they were each named after one of the assisting officers.

Harry was the first boy we photographed, so he was named after the first officer to check the situation, Harry Vitello. When I opened his carrier to let him out, he climbed up my shoulder, and held on to me tight. I felt so bad for him with his matted fur. I could feel that he had little muscle under that fur, and was dying to be loved. I photographed him, weighed him, vaccinated him, and placed him into the kennel where he would stay with the other boys for a few days. On Monday, March 30th, our veterinarian came in to examine the dogs. At that time, Harry weighed only 3.4 lbs., was dehydrated and really needed to put on some weight and muscle tone (not to mention needing a bath!). He also had a mouth full of rotting teeth. At that time, the vet determined him to be 8 to 10 years old. The vet suggested having him fostered until he was in a bit better shape, and I couldn't resist helping him since he would hold on to me more than any of the other Yorkies would. Harry came home that night, much to the dismay of my husband. After three weeks, I began showing Harry to prospective adopters. I heard many reasons why they didn't want to adopt him such as, "He's too old," "He likes you too much," "I don't know if I can housebreak him," and so on and so on. After the fourth week at my home passed, I had a dream that Harry was singing a song to me called "I'm Yours" by Jason Mraz. I took that as a sign and did the adoption papers the following day. About a week after I filled out the papers, my husband asked me, "When is he going back to the shelter? Never, right?" It was then that I told him that I did the paperwork the week before, and now Ed is just as in love with Harry as I am. I have never been this crazy about a dog, and I know that I am the center of his universe too. The bond that I share with him is amazing, it has just been a joy to watch him grow in the ways of the real world every day."

Nikki Thompson

149

rescued dogs

lessons from the road & rescue resources

Lessons from the Road
what I've learned from visiting rescues & shelters across the US over the last year

- **In many states, the law requires shelters to hold stray animals for 72 hours.** After that time, the dogs may be adopted out to other families or may be euthanized. Holding periods for strays are specified by state or local laws and the length varies from state to state. Some shelters elect to hold the animals for a longer period of time before making them available to the public. Only 30 percent of dogs that enter shelters are reclaimed by their owners.* Microchipping your dog and putting ID tags on your dog's collar are the best ways to ensure the unthinkable doesn't happen to your dog.

- **25 percent of all animals in shelters are purebred.*** In addition, there are hundreds of fabulous breed-specific rescues all across the country, doing amazing work for their favorite breeds (*see Blue Eyes, Bosco, Ginger, Gracie, Jaeger, Jasper, Jesse James, Lady (McNamara-Miller), Maggie, Martin, Mudd Puppy, Samantha, Sundance Kid & Taffy*).

- **Chihuahuas are the second most euthanized breed in California shelters.** Project Flying Chihuahuas (projectflyingchihuahuas.com) pulls them from California kill shelters and ships them to shelters in areas across the country where there isn't a surplus, and where they will have a better chance of finding a home.

- **Most dogs in pet stores are from puppy mills. In addition, some seemingly legitimate websites sell puppy-mill dogs.** If you buy one of these dogs, you are not rescuing a puppy-mill dog, but you are putting money into the hands of the people who own and operate puppy mills, and are thus perpetuating the system. Puppy-mill breeder dogs are often kept in deplorable conditions, walking on wire-floor cages that rip up the pads on their feet. They are never walked and urinate and defecate in their cages. Many have severe behavior and health problems. The cages are so small that many of these dogs, when finally freed, don't know how to walk in a straight line; they can only turn in circles (*see Darcy, Harry & Taffy; see pg. 149 for an account of a puppy-mill raid in Pennsylvania*).

- **Many hunting dogs are let loose in the woods after they "fail at hunting"** (*see Woody*).

- **The term "pit bull" is used to describe a number of breeds and mixed breeds that have a certain look.** Helen Keller owned a pit bull. The Little Rascal's Petey was a pit bull. Once referred to as nanny dogs in the US and UK, pit bulls are now banned and feared by many in both countries due to media hype. Many shelters don't adopt out pits and so they either euthanize them or ship them out to neighboring shelters. Some rescues reported to me that they couldn't get insurance to cover pit bull adoptions, so they don't take in pit bulls.

- **Large, black dogs have a more difficult time getting adopted and in some high-kill shelters are automatically euthanized. This is commonly referred to as "big black dog syndrome."**

- **Dogs should be judged as individuals** and not stereotyped and lumped into a category: pit bull, fight dog, shelter dog, deaf dog *(see Dena, Hector & Sadie).*

- **In some shelters, owner surrenders (dogs relinquished to shelters by their owners) are automatically euthanized.**

- **Most dogs are relinquished to shelters for reasons other than "my dog misbehaves."***** **Moving is listed as the top reason** (*see textbox*).

- **Money given to the HSUS and the ASPCA does NOT trickle down to your local Humane Society or SPCA**. If you want to help local animals, you need to donate directly to your local shelter or rescue.

- **The economy has caused an increase in animals in shelters across the US** (due to job loss, foreclosure, etc.). It has also caused a decrease in donations and a decrease in staffing at these facilities. Do what you can to help animals in your area by donating money or much needed items, such as food, or donating your time. Shelter animals benefit greatly from daily walks and interaction with humans. Helping to train a shelter dog could mean the difference between that dog getting a home or not getting a home. Your help will mean the world to each dog you help.

- **Dogs in kennels are not the same dog as dogs outside of kennels.** While some dogs do OK in shelters, most don't. They are terrified, understimulated, underexercised and stressed. Workers do what they can for these animals, but the environment is what it is. When walking through a shelter remember this and ask to take out even the animals you aren't so sure about. After a few minutes, they could show you their more relaxed side.

- Estimated number of cats and dogs entering shelters each year: 6-8 million*

- Estimated number of cats and dogs euthanized by shelters each year: 3-4 million* (approximately one animal every 8 seconds)

- Estimated number of cats and dogs adopted from shelters each year: 3-4 million*

- Estimated percent of owned dogs that were adopted from an animal shelter: 19 percent**

- Estimated percent of owned dogs that are spayed or neutered: 75 percent**

*The Humane Society of the United States (HSUS) estimate
**American Pet Products Manufacturers Association (APPMA) statistic from the 2009-2010 National Pet Owners Survey
***National Council on Pet Population Study & Policy (NCPPSP) statistic

Be a responsible pet guardian: microchip and put ID tags on your dog, train your dog, research breeds before you adopt, know the commitment you are making (a dog is for life), spay or neuter your dog
Help local animals: volunteer at or donate items or money to your local shelter

Resources
for information on...

"**Big black dog syndrome:**" Black Dog Rescue Project | blackdogrescueproject.com
Pet overpopulation: Best Friends Animal Society | bestfriends.org
Pit bulls: Animal Farm Foundation | animalfarmfoundation.org; BAD RAP | badrap.org; Best Friends Animal Society | bestfriends.org
Puppy mills: Main Line Animal Rescue | mlar.org; Best Friends Animal Society | bestfriends.org
Find local adoptable dogs: Petfinder | petfinder.com
Find local low- & no-cost spay & neuter programs: ASPCA | aspca.org/pet-care/spayneuter

the projects

In the days after I conceived of the idea for the projects back in August of 2008, I knew the undertaking could be so much more than a couple of books filled with photos of dogs. Sure, I could print two books, educate a few people and stop after that, but if I did that, how many people would my message reach, and wouldn't I be talking to the "already converted" anyway? It was then that I began to envision a series of books, each touching on a different topic affecting companion animals in the US today. People would be more likely to follow the series, and in the process, learn about topics that they previously had no knowledge of or interest in. I knew a series could reach a wider audience, and that just drove me to wonder how I could reach even more people. I thought of other avenues besides photo books. Maybe someone who wouldn't want a photo book on dogs could come across the projects through a photo gallery online, or see greeting cards at the grocery store and pick one up out of curiosity only to be touched by a dog's story on the back of the card. Those thoughts

led me to create the photo book projects not just as a couple of photo books on dogs, but as a series of photo books, gallery websites, prints, notecards and other items—all spreading the message, reaching people through a multitude of avenues and helping to educate the public on these important issues. That's when change starts to happen.

I can't exactly say that the production process for the first two books went smoothly (growing pains can be just that—painful!), but I can say that the whole experience was inspiring, humbling and rewarding. I started photographing for the first two books in the series, *Deaf Dogs* and *Rescued in America* in February 2009 and continued over a period of 14 months until April 2010. I like to say the photos went from A to Z, or rather from Alabama to Zeke—we went from our first photo session with Keller (*Deaf Dogs*) in Alabama, to our last photo session with Zeke (*Deaf Dogs*) in Florida. Photographing deaf dogs creates a set of challenges. A photographer can often get a hearing dog to look at the camera and cock his head to the side in a cute way by saying certain words or by squeaking a toy. This method obviously doesn't work with a deaf dog. While waving a hand or holding a treat will sometimes get a deaf dog's attention, it won't always get a cute expression. Add doggie vision problems to the mix and the photographer then needs to look inside herself to find patience she never knew she had.

There was no admission process for the first two books. Anyone in the US who wanted their deaf or rescued dog photographed for the books was accepted. Due to the overwhelming number of requests, I had to eventually shut my open-door policy. I did worry that this lack of an application process would result in a book filled with too many dogs from one part of the country or too many dogs of a certain breed, however, I think the final result was a nice mix of dogs. There is a large number of dogs from Maryland and Pennsylvania, but I'm from Baltimore and I live in Philadelphia, so I guess that is to be expected.

We took photos during a series of road trips across the US and held sessions in the participants' houses—in their living rooms, garages, dining rooms, family rooms, basements, kitchens, driveways and on their decks and patios. When we couldn't use the participants' homes, we borrowed their friends' homes for the day, or held sessions in one of the following: dance studios; firehalls; strip malls; dog-training facilities; doggie daycares; pet boutiques; paint rooms in auto-body shops; animal shelters; libraries; photo studios; universities and spas. When no other venues were available, as a last resort, we took photos outside. Studio shots were taken using just one or two softboxes and my old Canon. Space was often an issue. Cramming the photography equipment into someone's galley kitchen or small dining room created quite a challenge—especially when the room also needed to include a 135-lb. Great Dane.

Needless to say, under these circumstances, and with no funding, some things—among them my publication timeline for the books—didn't go as planned. On this page and the previous page are some photos from our road trips, as well as some "photo book project bloopers," including Milo (*Deaf Dogs*), who took a drink in a stream of mud during our outdoor shoot on a hot day in Florida, Joey (*Deaf Dogs*), who didn't realize the paper backdrop wasn't a sturdy white wall he could lean on, Miracle (*Rescued in America*), who had a case of stage fright, and the freak snowstorm in Tennessee that left us stranded along I-40 for over 4 hours.

Through all of the ups and downs, we have had a blast. Nothing beats traveling with Sadie on the open road. Nothing. She's the best travel companion ever. She takes on a road trip just as she takes on everything in life—with a sense of anticipation, adventure and a willingness to find fun wherever she goes. She and I have met some inspirational people and amazing dogs over the last year and a half. I'm grateful to every last one for their participation and help in making these books a reality. We can't wait to get on the road for next year's books.

Stats for both books:
Duration of photo sessions: 14 months (February 2009 - April 2010)
Number of road trips taken during that time: 25
Approximate miles traveled: 32,700
Number of states traversed during the trips: 44
Number of provinces traversed during the trips: 2
Number of states dogs were photographed in: 34
Number of provinces dogs were photographed in: 1
Total number of dogs photographed for both books: 183
Number of dogs photographed for *Deaf Dogs*: 78
Number of dogs photographed for *Rescued in America*: 105

Get your dog in the books!

Applications are now being accepted for people interested in having their pets photographed for future photo books.

Upcoming subjects: pit bulls, feral cats, puppy-mill dogs, senior dogs, tripods (three-legged cats & dogs), blind dogs & canine-cancer survivors, in addition to subsequent books on deaf dogs & rescued dogs

Visit www.thephotobooks.com
* to get information on the projects * to buy the books * to buy prints or cards of photos in the books
* to learn more about deaf & rescued dogs * to apply to have your dog or cat photographed for future photo books

rescues, shelters, websites

the following rescues, shelters & websites are responsible for saving the dogs in this book

all about animals | allaboutanimalsmacon.org
almost home animal shelter |
    petfinder.com/shelters/NJ445.html
american brittany rescue | americanbrittanyrescue.org
animal connections | petfinder.com/shelters/VA109.html
animal friends | thinkingoutsidethecage.org
animal friends humane society | animalfriendshs.org
animal friends rescue project | animalfriendsrescue.org
animal protection alliance |
    petfinder.com/shelters/MD141.html
animal welfare association | awanj.org
animals for life | animalsforlifect.org
arizona humane society | azhumane.org
aussie rescue & placement helpline | aussierescue.org
australian shepherd rescue page |
    aussierescue.leepfrog.com
baltimore animal rescue & care shelter |
    baltimoreanimalshelter.com
bay area doglovers responsible about pitbulls |
    badrap.org
bentley's buds great dane rescue |
    saveadane.webs.com
big dog rescue | bigdogrescue.com
bucks county spca | bcspca.org
canine crusaders | caninecrusaders.org
catahoula rescue inc | catahoularescue.com
catahoula united rescue society | catahoulaunited.com
central california spca | ccspca.com
central texas dachshund rescue | ctdr.org
c.h.a.t. adoption center of wakulla county |
    petfinder.com/shelters/FL479.html
deaf paws haven | petfinder.com/shelters/GA343.html
dogs deserve better | dogsdeservebetter.org
dogs for the deaf | dogsforthedeaf.org
dogsindanger.com | dogsindanger.com

ethical bull breed rescue & referral | ebbrr.org
4 paws for ability | 4pawsforability.org
german shorthaired pointer rescue pa | gsprescuepa.org
heartland golden retriever rescue |
    heartlandgoldenrescue.org
helping hands pet rescue | hhrescue.com
howard county animal control & adoption center |
    petfinder.com/shelters/MD106.html
humane society for animals | humanesocietyanimals.org
humane society of boulder valley | boulderhumane.org
humane society of elmore county | elmorehumane.org
humane society of st. joseph county |
    humanesocietystjc.org
maryland spca | mdspca.org
mixed up mutts | mixedupmutts.org
montgomery county spca | montgomerycountyspca.org
new england border collie rescue | nebcr.org
northeast georgia animal shelter | negas.weebly.com
orange county humane society | ochumanesociety.com
panhandle animal welfare society | paws-shelter.com
partnership for animal welfare | paw-rescue.org
petfinder | petfinder.com
philadelphia animal welfare society | phillypaws.org
pit rescue of the great plains | pitrescueofthegreatplains.org
ratbone rescues | ratbonerescues.com
saving furry friends | savingfurryfriends.com
saving shelter pets | savingshelterpets.com
saving the animals of rowan |
    petfinder.com/shelters/KY251.html
second time around rescue | secondtimearoundrescue.org
southland collie rescue | collie.org
southside animal shelter | ssasi.org
spca of northeastern north carolina | spcaofnenc.org
town lake animal center | petfinder.com/shelters/TX514.html
western pennsylvania humane society | wpahumane.org

sponsorships & dedications

the projects wish to thank the following individuals, businesses & organizations for their support

friends of the photo books sponsors

Bandit Austin, on behalf of his "bratty" sister, Missy Pooh Austin—Tacoma, WA

Wednesday Luria, Milo, Cutter & Johnnie, in memory of Cowboy—Hyattsville, MD

Egil Nilsson—Hartsville, PA

Catherine & Charles Rombeau, for Franklin & Rocky—Philadelphia, PA

The Skinner Family & the Copperline Crew—Attleboro, MA

silver sponsors

Michael & Allison Fanelli, in memory of Marino—Lansdale, PA

Trisha Spears & T-Bone—Crawfordville, FL

bronze sponsors

Amanda, Steven & Zuma Carlson—Arlington, VA

Steve, Toni & Georgia Carter, for Otis—*"See You in Heaven"*—Rogers, AR

Katherine Feldmann—*"You are in my heart forever, Marley & Murray"*

Susan & Patrick Lydem, in loving memory of Molly—Naugatuck, CT

Anne Mackenzie, for MacTavish, Myra & in special memory of Moonpie—Tallahassee, FL

Katie & Danny Shula, for Dottie—Marquette, MI

Grisha Stewart—Seattle, WA

Heidi Sydlosky, in loving memory of my Ace Monster—Elverson, PA

Judy Vorfeld—Peoria, AZ

Cheryl L Willoughby—Elizabethtown, NC

the following businesses, organizations & non-profits support the photo book projects

Amanda's Pet Care—Arlington, VA | amandaspetcare.com

AngelDogs Foundation, deaf dog rescue | angeldogsfoundation.org

Bellwether Events—Washington, DC wedding planning | bellwetherevents.com

The Big Bad Woof—Washington, DC | thebigbadwoof.com

The Catahoula Cookie Company—Tallahassee, FL | thecatahoulacookiecompany.com

Crunchies Natural Pet Foods—Crofton, MD | crunchies.com

Deaf Animals | deafanimals.org

Deaf Dog Connections, Advocacy, Resources & Education (D2Care) | d2care.org

Equinat-usa.com | equinat-usa.com

Internet Miniature Pinscher Service | minpinrescue.org

Pawsible Marketing | marketingmypetbusiness.com

Second Time Around Rescue—Chester Springs, PA | secondtimearoundrescue.org

special thanks to

egil nilsson
sadie
bella (for being a patient road-trip participant even when times got tough)
ann rea
debbie brown
gary crews & everyone at colorado printing
julie roads
peggie arvidson
tina austin
wednesday luria

the following businesses & organizations for hosting photo shoots:

animal friends rescue project	nashville fire department
animals for life	noblesville square animal clinic
bates college	northern plains boxer rescue
bell tower salon & medi-spa	paws pet boutique
the big bad woof	paws-itivly behaved k9's
bucks county spca	performance productions
corvettes etc	petsmart sioux falls
crunchies natural pet foods	pup 'n iron
dogone fun	st. hubert's dog training school
4 paws for ability	second time around rescue
must love dogs	stockman's supply

the bark magazine, deafanimals.org, dog art today, johannthedog.com, molly dendy, petfinder.com, petsit usa, urban dog magazine & zootoo.com for their pre-publication support of this book

the hundreds of people who pre-ordered the books because they believed in the projects & wanted to make the books a reality

the people lucky enough to be owned by the dogs in this book, who jumped on board to offer their dogs as participants, opened their homes to total strangers, pre-ordered books, offered their support & dealt with my ever-changing timeline

the shelters & rescues who supported & promoted the projects, especially american brittany rescue, animals for life, aussie rescue & placement helpline, bad rap, bucks county spca, d2care, dogs deserve better, dogs for the deaf, 4 paws for ability, magdrl, northern plains boxer rescue, paws in prison, second time around rescue

the sponsors for their belief in the projects, & a special thank you to the following business & non-profit sponsors: the big bad woof, d2care, equinat-usa.com